"فرِّش أسنانك! مشط شعرك!"
وبالرغم من أن سلاي كان يفعل الكثير
إلا أن أُمه لم تكن راضية أبداً.

كل نت أُم سلاي تصرخ دائماً:
"وضِّب غرفتك! إغسل الصحون!"

"Brush your teeth! Comb your hair!"
And however much Sly did, it was
never enough for his mum.

Sly's mum was always shouting:
"Tidy your room! Do the dishes!"

! فوكس

D___ _ly !

retold by

Henriette Barkow

illustrated by

Richard Johnson

Arabic translation
by Sajida Fawzi

MANTRA
LINGUA

وكانت الدجاجة الصغيرة الحمراء التي تسكن جوارهم تسمع كل شيئٍ.
وكانت تكره أن تسمع صراخ أُم سلاي وصياحها الدائم.

Next door Little Red could hear everything. She hated the way Sly's mum
always screamed and shouted.

وفي أحد الأيام سمعتها تصرخ وتقول :
"أُريد دجاجة مشويّة!"
وارتعبت الصغيرة الحمراء كثيراً.

One day she heard a scream:
"I want roast chicken!"
And Little Red became very
very scared.

وارتعب سلاي أيضاً، فهو لم يصطد دجاجة من قبل أبداً،
ولكنه فكر بخطة حيث أنه ثعلب ذكي.

Sly was scared too, he'd never caught a hen before,
but being a smart fox he had a plan.

وعندما خرجت الصغيرة الحمراء تَسَلَّلَ سلاي إلى بيتها
وبقي ينتظر و ينتظر، حتى عادت.

When Little Red went out Sly sneaked into her house and waited and waited, until she returned.

"النجدة! النجدة!" صرخت ا
لصغيرة الحمراء عندما رأت سلاي،
وقفزت إلى أعلى خزنة الكتب.
ولم يكن ذلك صعباً على سلاي،
فهو ثعلب وله خطة.

"Help! Help!" Little Red cried when
she saw Sly and jumped up onto the
top of the bookcase.
But that was no problem for Sly, after
all, he was a fox with a plan.

وبدأ سلاي يدور ويدور حول ذنبه.
وأخذ يسرع ويسرع حتى...

Sly started spinning round and round, chasing his tail.
Faster and faster he went until...

سقطت الصغيرة الحمراء في أعماق الكيس - ثمب!

وسحب سلاي الكيس إلى أسفل السُلّم- ثمبدي، ثمبدي بُم!

...Little Red fell down,   down,

down into the sack - THUMP!

Sly dragged the sack down the stairs - THUMPADY, THUMPADY, BUMP!

وعندما وصل الأرض شعر بتعب شديد ودوار وسرعان ما نام في أسفل السلّم.

By the time he reached the ground he was so tired and dizzy that he fell asleep at the bottom of the stairs.

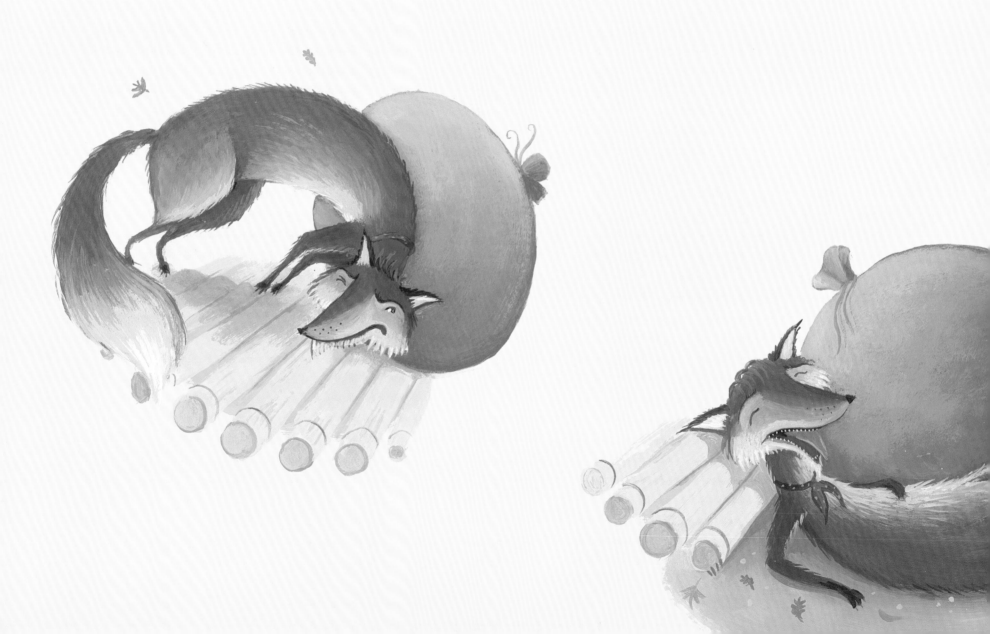

والآن حانت الفرصة للصعيرة الحمراء.

Now was Little Red's chance.

ضغطت على جسمها وخرجت من الكيس وصعدت
إلى أعلى، أعلى، أعلى، السلّم تركض بأسرع ما يمكن.

She squeezed herself out of the sack and ran as
fast as she could, up, up, up the stairs.

وعندما استعادت نشاطها أخذت الصغيرة الحمراء تفكر بسلاي المسكين والمتاعب التي يمكن أن تحصل له. ماذا تفعل لكي تساعده؟

When Little Red had recovered she thought about poor Sly and all the trouble he would be in. What could she do to help?

نظرت حواليها في المطبخ وجاءت لها فكرة.
أعدت دجاجة مشوية صنعتها من المواد النباتية في مطبخها.

She looked around her kitchen and then she had an idea.

وبعد أن انتهت أيقظت سلاي وأخبرته بخطتها .

When she had finished she woke Sly and told him of her plan.

وعاد سلاي إلى البيت يحمل
كيسه الثقيل.
وأعدّ مائدة العشاء ونادى أُمه.
"الدجاجة المشوية على المائدة،
تعالي و كلي!"

Sly went home with his heavy sack.
He made the dinner and set the
table, and then he called his mum.
"Roast chicken is ready, come and
get it!"

And did Sly's mum scream and shout?
She screamed with delight.
She shouted with joy: "That's the best
dinner I've ever had!"

وهل صرّخت وصاحت أُم سلاي؟
صرّخت مبتهجة وصاحت بسرور:
"هذا أحسن عشاء تناولته قط!"

ومنذ ذلك اليوم بدأ سلاي يُعِدُّ كل الطعام بمساعدة صديقته الجديدة.
وأما أُمه فلم تَعُدْ تُؤنبه إلاّ بين الحين والحين.

From that day forth Sly did all the cooking with the help of his new friend.
And Sly's mum, well she only nagged him now and then.

To the children of Mrs Michelsen's Class of 02
at Moss Hall Junior School
H.B.

For my friends, Rebecca Edwards
and Richard Holland
R.J.

First published in 2002 by Mantra Lingua Ltd
Global House, 303 Ballards Lane
London N12 8NP
www.mantralingua.com

Text copyright © 2002 Henriette Barkow
Illustration copyright © 2002 Richard Johnson
Dual language copyright © 2002 Mantra Lingua Ltd
This edition 2012